Newfound

Writers

Volume Two

Angles

of Life

2012

Ronald Collins, editor

O'CULLANE (COLLINS)

1st Edition – 2012

ISBN-13: 978-1470115562
ISBN-10: 1470115565

cover photo by
GC Photography and Video

Contents

Acknowledgment

We would like to thank

Kerrie Lynn Saraceno Collins

for her ideas, editing help and other forms of support.

Preface

This is the second volume of the Newfound writers series. The first volume, *Shadows of Water*, was focused on the work of local poets, but with this volume we have expanded the range to include prose and art.

This year our writers range from age fifteen to eighty-two, spring to autumn, so to speak.

In one case, that of writer J.N. the art and poems are so intertwined with each other that we scanned them in as one piece, so you can see them as the artist/writer created them.

The works are in alphabetical order by the poet's last name or initials.

The title *Angles of Life* was chosen because it seems the world has become edgier and sharper, with less forgiveness or caring, certainly less willingness to meet in the middle on issues that affect us all. Let us hope that this too shall pass.

Collins Publishing

Vin Broderick

Some Say the World Will End in Fire

The flame of autumn's leafy torch has not yet left the tree,
And red and yellow, gold and amber blaze the arbor sea.
But scarcely has the autumn's glow the summit of its prime
When silent shrouds of silver snow descend before their time.
The crystals do not douse the flames that dance upon the brush;
The flames do not dissolve the flakes that fall with gentle hush.
Instead the flake preserves the flame; it's crystallized and bright;
And flame ignites the neutral flake in brilliant firelight.
I have not tired of fall's hue; its colors thrill me still,
And snow, which hardly bores me now, by February will.
Each time has beauty of its own with different types of weather,
But neither has the glory shown of both seasons together.

Janice Dodd Collins

To Know

How do we know anything?
We study, observe,
question, always question.
There are no answers.
Yet we still question.
So much to learn,
that will never end.
Don't stop questioning.
Don't stop trying.
Don't stop learning.

Angles to Life

There are so many
where do we start?
Down one side,
down the other.
The sharp corners
are there too,
testing our ways,
testing our direction.
So fun to experiment.
testing each moment.
OK to be where you are,
to test the angles.

Here

The new, the old, the different,
we are all here together.
We all have a place,
a mission, a direction.
Each day may change this.
Each acquaintance may redirect us.
We are driven yet vulnerable.
Driven to make it better,
to keep it the same.
So lucky to have the choice,
So lucky to have the chance.
The best of all worlds.
The best place to be.

The Skies Over Paradise Point

So brilliant,
bright, vivid yet soft...
Sculptures and shapes...
Glows and shades...
They bring you peace,
quiet and calm,
a feeling of love.
Love of life
and all it brings.
A time to reflect,
appreciate and just linger
In the glory.

Mother's Day

I am so honored to be a Mom.
So loved and I love it all.
The grandkids are the highlight
but the kids are still the best.
Memories of when they were little and
all that we have been through.
The young ones a delight,
yet wild just like their parents.
Learning, living and becoming aware of
what life is all about.
So nice to be a Mom and a Mimi.

Hearts

You win the hearts of many,
earn their love,
relish in the glory
deserved, demanded, and enjoyed.
You take care of all our needs, desires and wishes.
This is easy for you,
so natural and real.
Cook, play, fix and feel.
You are the best
and hope your heart is filled.

A Challenge

Too much, yet invigorating,
stimulates the mind and soul,
gives energy,
gives meaning,
gives life.

Everyone needs a challenge.
Everyone needs life.
Challenge the mind, soul and body.
Don't resist – go after it.
Give what you can.
Take the rewards.
Enjoy life.
It has a lot to give.

Blowing

Life blows by,
can we catch a wave?
So much to encompass,
yet you really must try.
Catch the waves, wind and opportunities
and they will give you
a life to live for.

Jet Stream In The Air

Jet streams so distant
Yet give us a dimension
In the sky
Cool, still, yet
You know there is more
More to the world
More to life
The peace is still here
So treasured so real
Spoiled to the good life
Jet streams are still
A part of the real life
Thin, long and fading

What Makes You Feel?

Music, color, light, or flow,
life has so much
so don't miss it.
Feelings give you a depth.
Loving gives you true life.
Go to these depths,
feel the emotion,
let it form you .
It will give you a
beauty you have never known.
Let it flow,
BE YOU.

Legally Old

65+ Medicare and more,
I have made it.
Feels good yet feels strange.
Active, determined and driven.
Don't give up – don't give in,
Life is too good.
So much to learn, experience, and live, and give.
Still, the body says what and why.
Love every minute,
old is no fun and Mother Nature does no favors.
Enjoy – be tough – fight the pain.
Give all you can,
Legally old is OK.

The Present

Now, the present – all so good,
all that matters.
The past was OK,
live for the present,
enjoy the day.
The past provided the experiences,
the future gives you something to look forward to,
BUT the present is now,
will never be anything but now.
Don't let it go without the attention
it demands.
You can't repeat it,
it is lost after NOW.

Ronald W. Collins

Angles of Life

Life comes at us
from all sides.
Relentless,
merciless,
Life lives us.
Now this way
now that.
Life never stops,
 we do,
and much that
Life throws at us
and to us,
is because of us.
All the smooth
and sharp
angles of life.

Ice

Ice grips the lake
like need
grips our lives.
Our desires
and yearnings
are lost against
the glare
of our needs.
Need grips us
in our gut,
cold, burning cold,
and like the lake
we have no
way to loosen
it's grip.

Wind

Life forces our way
many things
not wanted
nor resisted for
being there.
We take what
comes blown our way
and do what
we can,
and often
what we must
to stand
against it.

Earth

The rocks
conceal us
eventually,
until then
we labor
to move them.
Roll them
up many hills.
Some protect us,
some pin us down,
and upon no rock
can we build
ourselves,
as all rocks
wear down
eventually.

Fire

I melt at times
from my own heat.
I generate it
over trivial things
that
when all is done
mean nothing.
       Heat me
       eat me as food
       burn me as an offering
       it is
       what fire is for.

Only do not think
you sacrifice anything.

Bear on the Porch

Last night it came
the bear that visits
my porch,
invading the bird feeders.
I heard a thump
and I had to check
and through the screen door
he stood and looked at me
and I at him.
Each knew he was caught.
If I had had a gun
he was dead,
and if he had wished
he could have easily
taken me through that thin door.
But both stood and stared,
each knowing the other,
we nodded
and went on
with our lives,
having shared this little
time together.

Change

Change is all there is.
If you are not changing
then you are dead.

Change is all,
embrace it!
The best and worst
things come through change,
and even if you
cannot control what
the next change will be,
it will be.

Those who cannot
bend with the winds
of change…
break.

Knut against the sea
is how you will be
to fight against change,
and those who cannot
change
will be broken.

A Walk in Hebron Woods

This path, who made it I wonder?
Where was the place he intended to go?
Now over grown used mostly by deer and moose,
the path seems to run from no certain spot
to some place now lost in woods.
It mattered then, for he who made it,
a great labor, so he could walk this path
for a purpose, like the man himself,
now lost and unknowable.

Butterfly

Newfound

It was new found
nearly three hundred
years ago
but only by those
newly here themselves.
The lake and forest,
the bobcat and wolf,
have been here
since the ice melted.
It is we who
are newly found,
and many of us
have found ourselves
here on it's
shore.

Frog

Point of View

The deer had less chance
than I realized
as the coyote closed in,
both slipping on the frozen lake.
From Paradise Point, through mist
and snow they came toward my shore.
At first a doe and fawn
I thought, but as they drew near
I saw the doe and then
the coyote I had thought fawn,
tearing at her flanks, nearly pulling her down.
My hackles up, to the lake edge
club in hand.
In the narrow water, between ice and land
she lay, the dog standing
over her, teeth bared and back up.
he stared at me and I him,
each knowing each,
we waited as death took the doe,
it's blood turning ice and water crimson.
Terror and sadness in the dog's eyes,
it needed the deer to survive,
and would I have done the same
if he lay there bleeding in the water?
"Take her" I thought, as I turned away,
and by doing so
let Nature be less troubled by.

Mom

It was warmer then.
Every day as I grew
she was there for me,
and beside me.
She was the strength
at home, it was her house.
Iron wrapped in burlap,
no velvet to be found.
Smart yet uneducated
except by life and love.
A presence felt by all
who enter her domain.
Now aged and frail,
feisty still, but hollow.
Hollow from the loss of him
and now from the loss
of herself. Memories and mind
deserting her when it
should be her time.
Years of sacrifice and
the only reward is
a mind quickly going.
Even those that love her
are being pushed away
as she fights a
losing battle with
herself.

Doing Time

Waiting is
all we seem to do sometimes.
Waiting to grow up,
waiting for love,
waiting to die...

Waiting with little things
that happen between the waits.
It is those little things
that matter the most,
are worth waiting for.

Curtain Call

We all have a last act.
Some men stand in war
and die,
some lie in a hospital
until they fade away.
Glory and peace,
chose your act
before it chooses
you.

Self Image

No man can be
who he wants to be,
the 'who' is now
and tomorrow
it will be a
different who,
as I will be a
different me
for a little while,
until, that is,
I want to be
a different who
in a different now.

Shapes

Clouds shape themselves
around motions in the air
we cannot see.
We at times
shape ourselves around
emotions we can't acknowledge,
and like clouds
we become caught
in motions we can't
control,
nor want to.

Metamorphosis

I am not the man you know
and tomorrow I will be
a different man than today.
Life changes us
and, I wonder,
do we change life,
as our differences
are passed to our
children and grandchildren?
Probably so,
and they, will not be
as we know them now
tomorrow.

Scientific Truth

Remember the first time
you saw the light?
It was everywhere
even where we did not look
to see it.
It grew as we did.
How strange
that others cannot
see.
It is right there
to be seen
for those
who have
eyes that are open.

Duet

We are two
just you and me,
and when it is
more than us
it seems to be less
us.
Others come,
some stay too long,
but eventually
it is just us
and how I love it so.

Searches

Our models are all we have.
Reality, directly and fully known
is not for us. Only our models of it.
And those we tweak, make better,
maybe even complete someday,
but Oh, how I would love to
know, really know, the world
as it truly is.

We, as humans, are the limit
of knowing. What lies
beyond our senses and
imagination, we can only
model. We are model
dependent beings
created in our own image.

Reflections of an Old Mind

I wander tonight
into realms of my own creation.
Some are about love.
Some about shadows on the cave walls.
Which, I wonder,
matter the most
or matter at all.
Love,
of course love,
how else,
but the others,
science, reality,
ontological musings,
do I really need them?

Yes, I do
they are a part of me
as much as love is.
All here and
I would not be
without them.

Living Instead

Life lives us
as it has countless other creatures
great and small.
We live on its terms,
restricted to its needs.
We enjoy the life
given to us
but we know we are
only temporarily here,
and when we pass
life will not care,
but simply move on
to the next
form of which
we are but one.

Hidden Strength

Deep roots are not touched
by the frost,
and the strength they provide
are the hidden strength
we all need.

Roots come in many forms:
In family, in friends,
in ourselves
when we allow ourselves
to be who we are.

Roots make us strong
but do not hold us in place.
They support us
not restrict who we are.
Enjoy, and appreciate your roots.

Priorities

Our priorities change as we age,
I remember when what I looked like
was more important than how healthy I was.
Who I was with was more important
than my enjoyment of being with them.
Showing off what I had and had done
was more important than enjoying
those willing to share it with me.
Now less, and each year even less,
mean much to me.
Certainly my love and friends
and family are what really matters to me.
Most else has faded in significance
and I have grown the more
because of it.

The Journey

From where we began
how did we come
to this day?

We are not what
we thought we would be
when we started this journey.

So how is this day possible?
How could we be here
from where we began?

Many roads we stepped on
but the ones we strode
led to here, now, to us.

Down from where we began
the roads lead to many places
and we, we chose the only ones
that arrive at you and me.

The Path Taken

Far from where we began
through love, toil and pain
we have come to here
where we are together.

How strange the road has been
with its many twists and turns
its many surprises, some good
and some we'd like to forget.

We walked the many paths,
most unseen until we were
upon them and unable to change
even if we had wanted too.

Did we chose the paths
or did we take the path we had too?
Who had the sight to see
where they all could lead?

Some seemed so right
and proved to be so wrong.
We are wary now of all paths
that you cannot get off
once you step upon them.

Unintended Consequences

It is the unintended consequences
that hurt us.
The quick decision,
the easy path or hard,
later lead to more pain
than they cured.

No one can see the end
of all things, cannot see where
what seems right or wrong now
will lead.

Be not too fast nor too hard
to judge
what seems obviously wrong
today
may prove before the end
to have been
the right thing
to have done.

Ents

During a long life
you learn things
that you wish to share
but just when you are
old enough to see the wisdom
you have earned
you are too old
to be accepted as knowing
enough to be asked
by those who need it.

Life's Dance

Life is not planned
nor does life just happen.
You lay out the parts you can,
an education, even a career,
but these are not the parts
that matter the most.
The important parts happen
when you least expect them,
and you need to be ready,
to go with them or to move aside.
It is the unplanned
that have the most impact,
are felt the most,
both pleasure and pain,
both unplanned and unavoidable.

James Crawford

Wishes For Mallory

Welcome to this world, Mallory, a world that is already a better place with you joining us.

Did you come from heaven? I think you must have. For although you've been here only two months, you've already made a positive change in this grandfather's view of life on this earth. That sense of change is strongest when I'm holding you and don't want to let go.

Some say a newborn is evidence of God's intention that the world should go on. I say you are also proof that He will continue to grace our world with beauty.

There are so many things I wish for you. But first let me point out that the biggest wish for every child has already been granted in your case: You have parents who could not be more caring, loving or protective. The bond they feel with you is so compelling that there will come a time, if it hasn't already, when they will gaze down upon you in wonder as you sleep. And it is then that a sense of overwhelming personal responsibility for your wellbeing will wash over them; an awareness of how precious yet vulnerable you are; a realization that you are totally dependent on them for your safety and for meeting all of your needs as you grow.

That profound feeling can be unnerving but is a natural rite of passage for loving parents and will not persist. Nor should it, in the case of your mother and father, for they have without question every attribute needed by those who wish to be the best parent possible.

So why did I tell you this? Because I hope you will see that moment in your mind as you grow, and realize –

especially when you might be tempted to criticize them – just how daunting a task they took on for you.

Now the wishes…

I wish you fame: Not famous to the world; that just brings envy, critical scrutiny and loss of privacy. Rather, the greater fame among your family and friends as someone who can always be counted on to be there for them.

I wish you empathy: The capacity to recognize when others aren't able to lift themselves up, and the will and means to help them.

I wish you humor: A broad sense of humor that will help sustain you in difficult times while also enabling you to enjoy one of life's most valuable offerings – shared moments of laughter with family and friends.

I wish you the power of a positive outlook: To be relentless in looking for the positive aspect of every situation, no matter how bleak the circumstances. To search for the opportunities that are almost always found within problems, and to avoid people who dwell on the negative. For there is a bounty of good and beauty to be found in this world. To turn away from it, or worse, to view it as alien or irrelevant, is merely inviting melancholy to intrude on what should be a joyous celebration of wonder.

I wish you patience: The serenity to wait while a sunset moves through all stages of its glory. The strength to wait and learn more before reacting; to resist the temptation to stereotype others or categorize issues as black or white, without acknowledging the gray or hearing the other side.

I wish you modesty: The ability to laugh at yourself; to not worry about who will get the credit (so that you and others can achieve more together); to readily acknowledge what you don't yet know; and to welcome suggestions from others without faulting yourself for not thinking them first.

I wish you courage and confidence: You will have the great advantage of parents who will have given you the knowledge and support you need to deal with any challenge. And understanding usually prevents fear. So you might respect, but have no reason to fear, any social, academic or business situation. Try not to worry; otherwise, during your lifetime you could suffer through countless catastrophes, disasters and tragedies, nearly all of which will never occur.

I wish you determination: To persevere to completion when you know what you're doing is right, no matter how many doubts or obstacles are raised by others.

I wish you love: The singular experience of loving and being loved by a spouse and family and friends. I hope you also enjoy the less intense but nevertheless important form of love – sharing greetings, events and compliments with other people you meet, however briefly.

I wish you no regrets: Please always remember that no one can go back and make a new beginning, but anyone can start today and make a new ending.

So walk barefoot every chance you get... see the shapes in the clouds... lie in a hammock ... gaze at the majesty of the oceans and mountains... explore... dream... discover... and, above all, have fun.

One final wish, and this one's for me. I wish for many years to share with you. But even after I've gone, I'll be watching over you and helping you in every way I can.

So long for now, Mallory. God bless you.

All my love,
Grampy

The Town Meeting Will Now Come To Order

Please...Pretty Please?

It's Town Meeting Time in the Lakes Region!

If you've never attended one before and are about to make the leap, here's a guide to what you can expect.

First, arrive early to get a seat. Many town meetings are held in quaint historic buildings with only enough chairs for seven saloonkeepers, five blacksmiths and four witches. And whatever you do, don't sit beside someone who is scrutinizing the annual report, especially if he's making margin notations. Later, when he enters the fray, you won't want anyone to think you came with him.

The meeting will often extend over several nights (no, you don't sleep over). Discussions will be led by a Moderator who, on average, will lose control of the meeting 38.4 times.

Here are some typical warrant articles and what you can expect for discourse:

To see if the Town will vote to raise and appropriate the sum of $20,000 to fix the potholes on South Main Street. The Moderator asks for any discussion. A man in his 80's elbows others who wish to speak out of the way and grabs the microphone. He's reminded twice to give his name, to which he growls, "Hell, everybody here knows me."

His remarks are delivered slowly, so agonizingly slow that many attendees are soon hanging their heads between their knees and wringing their copies of the annual report into balloon shapes. He drawls, "Now I know most of you folks weren't around back in the 40's...well, maybe Clem over there...and Herb, maybe...Herb, were you workin' at that fillin' station back then?... No? I coulda sworn you were....

"Anyway, I'm here to tell ya that we had real potholes back in them days.... Not the baby holes you're all talkin' about here, that are maybe a foot deep and three long....No sir, back then we had potholes that swallowed tractors whole.... Monster potholes.... Hell, they're the reason these teeth aren't my own. (Laughter erupts, eyes roll, the Moderator bangs his gavel.) But we learned to live with 'em....Let me tell ya what you do – it's very simple...."

After every five minutes the Moderator tries to cut him off. Each time, he answers with something like, "Now, son (the Moderator is 55), you just hold your horses. You seem to think this is one big circus and that I'm just one of the clowns. You need to show a bit more respect for us taxpayers." Before he finally sits down, he ends with: "And by the way, Mr. Chairman of the Selectmen, you need to get us out of Afghanistan. Now."

To see if the Town will vote to raise and appropriate the sum of $13,354,000 for removal of polybenzenes and hydrosynthetics from the former genetics site, through the application of third-generation, nonspecific microbial organisms. The Moderator invites discussion. No one gets up to speak. In truth, no one has any clue on this warrant article. The Town Engineer, who flunked chemistry and biology, breathes a huge sigh of relief when no questions are asked of him. It passes by voice vote.

To see if the Town will vote to allow use of the Town Hall for a ping-pong tournament to benefit a local orphanage. Even before the Moderator asks if anyone wishes to speak to this article, the line for the microphone snakes out the door and down to the interstate.

Six mothers, one after the other, argue that players will "put their eyes out" or suffer concussions from wayward paddles; one thinks her cousin told her the paddle handles cause cancer. Someone suggests that Nerf balls be mandated. Another speaker is adamant that the games should be played to 21 points, not 15. Someone demands certification that the

58

orphans are indeed orphans. Another speaker claims studies show "ping-pong invariably attracts the gambling element and all that comes with it – prostitution, drugs, muggings, the whole lot."

The man who before the meeting was making margin notes in the annual report tries to point out that there will be no cost to the Town and that it's for a worthy cause. The crowd showers him with a cacophony of boos, hisses, hoots, and shouts of "Sit down!" and "Who asked you?" Bent over to shield himself from the verbal hailstorm, he exits the building through a side door to a chorus of Bronx cheers. The meeting votes to table the issue to the following night with the stipulation that at least two orphans be made available then for questioning.

To see if the Town will approve those portions of the operating budget that fund the Water and Sewer, Police and Fire Departments.

One resident wants to know where the Water and Sewer people were when his toilet overflowed. A speaker complains that firemen who arrived before him copped the last six chocolate crullers at the local Dunkin' Donuts that morning.

A retiree who lives across the street from the local supermarket reports that every day she observes the same selfish person hoarding some 30 shopping carts and bringing them all into the store with him, apparently with no thought to whether some other shopper might need one. She wants to know what the police intend to do about it, there's nothing wrong with her eyesight, and she's willing to testify in court, but only before that nice Judge Wapner.

A fed-up taxpayer known also as a shady character questions whether the police are using the fitness equipment the town spent $10,000 on three years ago. Citing the Fifth Amendment in refusing to give his name, he says Burglar

Magazine (which he insists he was reading in a doctor's office) recently ran a reader poll on "The Easiest Cops To Outrun" and several local cops finished near the top in the voting.

Someone then points out that "Dancing With The Stars" will be on in 10 minutes. Motions for adjournment ring out from all corners of the hall. The gavel comes down and all rush for the exits. Some 23 drivers, in their haste to take a shortcut home, race down South Main Street and suffer serious front-end damage from potholes.

I hope this guide has been helpful and that you will now participate in a Town Meeting with no fear of making a fool of yourself.

J.N.

#14

The wonder is you never know
When you open your eyes
What new surprises, visible or hidden
are waiting there for you to find.
Perhaps you noticed I didn't say
"When you awaken"
"Open eyes" while closed in sleep
Still keep what they have seen
And show them to you as they will
refreshed by innovations in a dream

#15

In flickering flight
Faster and more fantastic
Than the path of a symphony baton
The swallow dips and dives in air
Above the waters of the lake
Feasting on winged fare
Almost too small to see
Until she meets her own sharp eyes
Staring back at her
From water's shine
And that sends her diving skyward
In a plumb-line streak

We see them almost anywhere
Giant granite eggs
Laid by the groaning glacier
Probing thru a shuddering terrain
Eons past remembering
Here to remain for Indian eyes
To discover and Indian fingers
To chisel with history and mysteries
To name and to approach with
Solemn reverence
    We see them almost everywhere
    And wonder -
Deep within their·stony hearts
Do they remember

The bare white birches over there
Along the Lake's far verge
Are faultlessly reflected
In still water
Precise as anyone could wish
     But what I see
     I do believe is the
Delicate skeleton of a fish
Intact upon a green-glazed dish

#18

Spring sows FIDDLEHEADS
By scores of scores
But never once has she been known
To pluck a hidden violin
From beneath the mucky snow
Tuck it under her dainty chin
And play a solo fine and clear
To waken Dawn or summon Night
      Oh dear me no
She much prefers an accolade
From Cheepers, Peepers, Croakers
And Beepers that come to name her
"QUEEN OF SEASONS"
Which may be true
      Though some dispute it

#19

Snow flocked islands of ice
Rise and fall
Upon the lake's cold breast
In respiration rhythm
While tired ducks vie
For rest space in between
And have but little opportunity
To sleep
And dream of flight to warmer climes

Swathed in diaphanous gossamer
Worn to grace her lovers tryst
The lulled lake
Languidly awakens
And waves a misty hand
To fleeing Night
Too soon her gentle
Love - surfeited sigh
Is banished by imperial Sun
Who plucks the gauzy drapes away
To claim her naked
For the day

#21

The last one leaving
Forgot to close the boathouse door
All winter long it hangs agape
In one protracted rictus yawn
While in its throat
A desolate disgruntled boat
Thumps with every ripple
Bumps with every wave
Rubs and chafes and makes a sound
Monotonous as a snore

#22

```
The guttering breath
Of in-rushing wind
Makes the forest an oboe orchestra
No chance today of competition
From drum boom-booming surf
For it was silenced overnight
It's rigid fists bewitched by winter
Hang poised to strike the final tones
Which no one now will hear
This year
```

#23

The soggy drifts of ends of odds
and odds of ends
That clogged the frowsy sands
Were whisked away by wind and rain
To be replaced with a daring new design
Festoons and leafy wreaths
Gold bronze and crimson intertwined

#24

These were its dimensions
Accurate I assure you
Picture it a circle
Six inches in diameter
Imagine it's a fine white mushroom
Now see it on a carpet of moss
        "If you will"
And observe the pine nut seeds
Arranged as a formal setting
        It's very sad - if true
But I believe my rude intrusion
Put to flight
A chipmunk rendezvous

#25

The face of the sun
We cannot see
But radiant beams announce his coming
Cherubic pink-cheeked clouds
Frolic over the distant hills
Not stern and granite grey
As you might think
But glowing now
A nipple pink

Chunky clouds
Grey as earthen clay
Take shape in the hands
Of a burly wind
No artist this one
            Whose sole intention
Is to pound and pummel
Squeeze out thunder
Slash asunder and fling to earth
A terrifying jagged lance
He forged therein

#27

Tipsy Bob-houses utter sloshy serenades

In praise of early Spring

For she has set them footloose

And fancy free to jostle one another

In reckless revelry!

#28

Careening whorls of scurrying leaves
Drunk with colors
Claret sherry burgundy chablis
tease and tug at the reluctant ones
Timidly clinging to the sapless boughs
Until the wind returns to grab them by
the fistful and fling them fluttering
Against hedgerow fence and wall
Where wedged in close embrace
They will remain asleep the winter away
Beneath the snow

#29

Glassy fingers point and beckon
Along the shoreline
Of the restive lake
These once were waves
Alive
And clutching at the sand
See them now transfixed
and frozen hand in hand

#30

```
Is it an illusion
That motion high above the mist
Were those really wings I glimpsed
Beating with the rhythm of my heart
Or perhaps the spirit of a species
Lost to time
Is the answer mine to know
I wonder
When suddenly above and starkly clear
A cruciform appears
No less transfixing
Than the vision
Although I know it now by name
It is a crane
```

#31

Big houses full of furniture
But empty now of voices
Stare blindly at the lake
And wait for another summer
So no one will mind - I hope
If I scramble along the water's verge
Of their Private Properties
And filch a special stone or two
A sand-scoured fantasy of driftwood
Or a flame-carved piece of sculpture
For my own

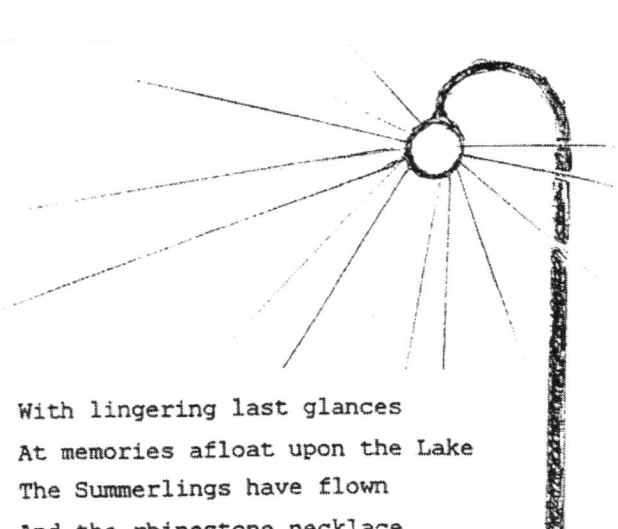

With lingering last glances
At memories afloat upon the Lake
The Summerlings have flown
And the rhinestone necklace
Night has worn is no more
So now she comes quite unadorned
But for a few dim solitaires
And even these she tucks away
Before we slumber

Sheila Oranch

Web of Life

What wonder winds this subtle silk,
With kith and kin, icon and ilk?

What a ragged gaping fearful lapse,
Jet cast to cause our dream's collapse!

Broke not, the pattern only bends,
Bridged with hope, by Love it mends.

(9/27/2001)

High Kicking Spirit

Ostrich isn't very poetical.
Yet the daddy is often heroical.
He nurtures and guards and teaches the chicks.
When guiding his flock at nothing he sticks.
So stretch out your neck and crank up your nerve,
And attack your dreams with some vigor and verve.
'Cause the world needs your vision and passion and love,
And your high-kicking spirit those mountains will shove.

I Keep the Picture

Tan and age-spotted, gnarly knuckles shiny like the top of his head. Eyes that twinkle and mouth with a quirky smile.
Sitting quietly waiting, hands resting on the table, watching people come and go. In no hurry, with no compelling anxieties to pursue. The train will come when it comes.
May I share the table? Of course, if I like. Life is funny, and we talk about coming and going.
I tell him about what a hard time my family gives me, and he comforts me.
He tells me about being alone and I comfort him. Nothing we want from each other or need.
No demands or judgments.
I miss my gramps. Can I adopt him? I can barely take care of myself yet.
We ask the waitress to take our picture.
Smiling with our heads leaned together we look intimate and important to each other.
The train comes and I leave. I don't know his name but I keep the picture.
I still have the picture in my album.
People always ask who that wonderful old man is.
I don't know, but we sure were happy with each other for a little while.

Dappled Day

Imperfections dapple the day
A phone too loud
An envelope missed
Chin hairs grew
Offset by sweet spots
The baby walked
A cutting sprouted
An old friend called
I love my dappled day

Bumblebee Soup
(a two part chant)

Little Chantal was playing in the bath,
Mixing up some bubbles with a splash, splash,
splash!
"What are you making with your bowl and spoon?"
Grandma asked Chantal, "Will it be done soon?"
"Soup! I'm making soup. And it's ready right now."
"Try some, Grandma, it's yummy good chow."
In walked Grandpa, and was offered some soup,
"Try some, Grandpa, it's just for you."
"What kind of soup should I try, Chantal?"
"Bumblebee soup, Grandpa, take a smell."
"Bumblebee, yuck, I can't eat that!"
"Sure you can, it won't make you fat."
She said,
"Eat the bumblebee, eat the bumblebee,
Eat the bumblebee, eat the bumblebee!"
And he said,
"Way out in the woods where the big bears go,
There's a little song that they all know.
When they climb up the trees to get some honey,
They sing this song and it sounds kinda funny,
They sing,
"Eat the bumblebee, eat the bumblebee,
Eat the bumblebee, eat the bumblebee!"

Don't Bother Your Mind

Whitebreasted Nuthatch
Elegant design
Specialty product
Function refined

Religious or Natural?
Don't bother your mind
Because God's solution
IS evolution!

Frost's First Fling

(for Robert Frost)

Today we awaken to Frost's first fling,
Magical gloss on ordinary things.
Vegetable nightmare,
Artist's delight.
Let's find snowy woods
To stop by tonight

Juliet Elizabeth Pruden

Selfishness

I needed you to hold me
To keep me safe from the world,
And you,
And myself
Because I can hide in your arms
Scorning the truth and my state of mental health.

For I know we are not meant to be together
But cannot cut myself loose.
I'm caught in a web you've spun,
A lover hangman's noose.

What of my strength, my conscience?
Their fire has burned low,
Nearly extinguished
By the depth in your sea-blue eyes.

Solace sweeps over me,
Like that melodic and captivating Scott Joplin tune,
When I awaken beside you,
Our bodies entwined and beautiful.

The sun creeps in and kisses your shoulder, lips, and brow
Like I so long to do
Every time I see you.
Some part of your body and being
                                        Reached out

And (ensnared) mine
And to deny that desire for you
Would be to deny my happiness,
Something I am not wont to do.

As twilight takes shape,
My soul fills with passion.
The breeze strikes up and thunderheads SWELL
This drive, as insistent as a pulse,
To be with you, part of you.
Now, how can you refuse me—
Leaving me to endure such a hollow ache?

Then hurt masquerades as anger,
Dancing madly at a ball,
Cheek to cheek with selfishness,
When it should just be you and I
Together that way,
Two lovers alone generating their own beat
Compelled by deep instincts and hunger for each other.

So why won't you hold me
And keep me safe from the world,
And you,
And myself?
Because I can hide in your arms,
Believing only what I want and nothing else.

Hard to Keep

Sometimes it is so hard not to tell you
The words that I feel so well
They would fall harsh and dissonant on your ears
Like an early alarm clock or an old country song
Something you are not ready to hear or would like to turn off

Yet they fill me with joy and hope
A sense of purpose
For in your arms only am I fully at peace
Lying next to you—warm, naked, and secure
Secretly cherished

So I try to tell you soundlessly
And wonder if you are blind too?
Can you not see the love in my eyes
Feel the tenderness in my touch
Sense the serenity in my body by your side
You're home, safe from the battles now

Open your eyes
And open your soul
Don't be afraid
I'll hold you close
And kiss away the fear

It won't hurt
I want to heal your wounds
Make you whole again
Make you feel again
Make you love again—me.

"Just Beyond the Edge of the Woods"

"Just beyond the edge of the woods,
You'll find it there," the voice whispered.
"But how will I know when I've found it?" I replied.
The voice came again, "Just be open."
And so I sought out the spot
Drawn by curiosity and desire
But somewhat hesitant, for this was real.
All senses heightened and skin prickly,
I noticed the greens how they gleamed
And the blue how it sparkled.
The silence and presence of the forest
Enveloped me,
Held me like a lover,
And I gave myself to it;
A pledge for my life
Attuned to the earth, air, water and fire.
I'll learn the dances of fairies,
The songs of the sirens,
The games of the elves,
And the flights of the pixies.
I'll talk to the animals,
Laugh with the children,
Live without regrets,
And love without caution.
I'll worship the Moon
In all of Her phases
And cherish the Sun too.
"Just beyond the edge of the woods"
Who knew?

95 and Counting

I don't think it possible
To know all at once
What we will lose
When you leave this earth
There will be the initial sadness
And family comforting to be done
The hope that your soul
Is in comfort and at peace
The relief that you no longer feel pain
And that gladness that you're with
Your sweetheart again
But I think the losses
Will poke at us over time
In small ways and unexpectedly
Old memories will surface
And questions will arise
That now will have to go unanswered
A long life lived
And much that you'll leave behind
But still so much you'll take with you

In remembrance of Mary Elizabeth Werner, my grandmother
4/22/09—1/27/08

The Midnight Walkers

'Twas nearly the hour for us, the midnight walkers,
Restless in the bar amidst the smoke, the smell of beer,
and the inebriated talkers.
On a seemingly normal, innocent night
The stars had popped out, and the moon was shining bright.
We midnight walkers, taking libation,
Sat at the bar and lapsed into conversation.
We came seeking friends we'd already made—
For one of us, eight years' worth of tales to trade.
The fates were there too, perched on three bar stools,
And we all know, they don't play by the rules.
So, instead, we found the writer among us
Hovering, just there, between Juli and Russ.
Our original intents began to lose shape,
And the writer among us shook on his cape.
"Amazing," we marveled, "the bonds that we share."
And decided to take a little night air.
We midnight walkers strolled out of the bar
And retrieved a willing dog from inside the car.
We four headed down to the shoreline below,
None of us caring in which direction to go;
So long as we could walk and talk, winding our way
Through the paths and piers before the light of day.
And the writer among us was entertained,
He listened to everything and spoke unrestrained.
A tour through the dark and histories shared,
The hour was late, but not a one cared.
We midnight walkers, we walked and we wandered—
Not a thought wasted, not an idea squandered,
Down the murky lanes on our muddy soles,
On lookout for bears with midnight snacks as goals.

And the writer among us was delighted to meet
Another who marched to a different beat.
We journeyed on, loath to separate.
The writer among us did not want to wait
Until a time, not yet known,
When we could all be – together alone.
But the three fates, as unjust as they may be,
Would surely not unite us, without some future plan, you see.
So for now, we midnight walkers—We'll walk away,
But the writer among us will bind us, day after day.

For Russ--a fellow midnight walker.

composed 4/13/03 along the Shore Path, Bar Harbor

As a Spanish teacher, every year at the beginning of November, I got to share with students customs surrounding Mexico's Day of the Dead or El Día de los Muertos. In Mexico, death is something that is a natural part of life and faced head-on. Rather than fear it, it is something that is personified, as evidenced by all of the skeletons in their art, and also mocked. Kids delight in purchasing candy skulls with their own names printed on them and eating Pan de los Muertos, bread of the dead and getting to find the ornamental bones baked into the bread. There is a religious component of remembrance and honor as well, creating shrines to dead relatives and visits to the cemetery. To help my students embrace the humor and acceptance with which the Mexicans treat death, each year I asked them to write a humorous poem about a death, their own or a pop-culture figure, or that of somebody they knew (with that person's permission.)

El Poema del Día de los Muertos
Escrito por Srta. Pruden

There once was a Spanish teacher at KHS
Poor Señorita Pruden, she tried her best
But her Block 4 class really put her to the test

In the early afternoon on every blue day
They'd come pushing and shoving everyone out of the way
Just like a bull charging into the ring, OLÉ

They'd forget to spit their gum out at the door
With their homework made paper airplanes to litter the floor
It's no wonder Señorita Pruden is no more

They tortured that poor woman, that motley crew
Mispronouncing their h's and double l's too
Traipsing around the room like it was some kind of zoo

We'll always remember her pulling out her hair
Repeating nunca, nunca, nunca, Don't you dare,
And Pedro would you please stay in your chair

That class was a horror, there is no doubt
It stank of cologne—Margarita would shout
Gregorio listened to his discman, and Marcos was always conking out

The other's sins were too numerous to mention
I assure you this story is no invention
Those kids should spend their lives in detention

And so it came to an end that fateful day
Poor Señorita collapsed to the ground and there she lay
The Block 4 kids just shrugged at each other and said ¿Por qué?

There will never be another quite like her, we know
Although she could haunt us, I'm afraid so
I mean, killed by a Spanish class, what a way to go!

And so in the dark of night if you hear
Mt. Dew being opened and Spanish whispered in your ear
It's only Señorita Pruden, have no fear

~

Dedicated obviously to my Block 4 class,
And especially to Pedro for thinking to ask,
"Señorita Pruden, did you complete this task?"

Why I can't write...

There's nothing like procrastination
But it's not for lack of motivation
Pressing obligations taking charge
Wish the mortgage weren't as large

Guest rooms to clean
Grass still long and green
The phone keeps ringing
And the doorbell's a-dinging

No time to sit and write
Dinner's not until 10 at night
Bedtime's not until 2
There's just so much to do

New piano students to assess
Gosh this kitchen's quite a mess
Several dance classes to design
Are you sure these jobs are all mine?

Yuletide craft show spaces to fill
Writing? Aren't there a few weeks still?
Laundry to prewash and load
I think my brain's starting to corrode

No time to sit and write
Dinner again at 10 at night
And going to bed at 2?
Not me, there's just too much to do.

[This was an "assignment" during the "Your Life Preserved" Writers' Workshops held at Six Chimneys & A Dream to face head-on the things that prevent us from writing.]

[Both "Wendell's Girl" and "The Summer of '55" were written during the Preserving Your Life writers' workshops held at Six Chimneys & A Dream. The focus of which was to record family and personal stories for the insight into the characters and also for the enjoyment of current and future generations. Thanks to the other members of the group for their valuable feedback as my stories went through the revision process.]

Wendell's Girl

I have always had a gift and an ear for music, and I was fortunate to be born into a family that valued cultural experiences. We attended concerts and recitals that exposed us to different instruments and styles of music. I began to play the piano when I was four, but as I progressed through elementary school, classical music did not excite me, did not move me. I could play any pop music I wanted to because I have perfect pitch, and I could pick it up off the radio. The strict piano teachers didn't consider that serious music, nor would my mother pay for lessons on something that frivolous. They kept pushing classical music. I kept trying to quit. I found tactics to defeat the thirty minutes a day of practice time that my mother set on the oven timer. I suddenly developed a powerful thirst or had to go to the bathroom as a result. I even reached the point where I could read a book while playing songs I knew well. My mother either didn't catch on or was tired of fighting with me, more likely the latter. However, she refused to let me quit taking lessons until I reached the age of fifteen. As I got older and was able to do more with my music, I quit fighting so hard. I still had to play classical music for lessons, but I started to accompany the school chorus and friends at their band auditions with a wider range of music. My practice time increased to 45 minutes a day, and I'm sure my mother breathed a sigh of relief. What's more—I discovered what I really wanted to play.

From the first time I ever heard Dixieland music, it held me enthralled; the sweet harmonies, the counterpoint of drums, bass fiddle, piano, clarinet, banjo, and the brass, sometimes tuba, always trombone, but then that trumpet, that sassy trumpet. No matter whether in the tiny, dark confines sitting on the floor of Preservation Hall in N'awleans or a large symphony center filled with plush seats and people, it was just me and that music, weaving its way into my soul. There was no longer any question after that first trip to N'awleans at the age of 13, that what I really needed to play was ragtime, the closest thing to Dixieland that didn't require a band. Watching Sweet Emma pound those keys, making that old upright shake, affirmed that this was not just the music of old black men with enormous hand spans; little old women could rule this domain as well. And what if I became one of them?

I entertained thoughts of going to Juilliard, but I did not want to devote my existence to practicing endlessly. I'm not sure the music professors approve of ragtime pianists either. Certainly I might have played on Broadway; I have no doubt I am good enough, but how does one get those gigs without the proper credentials? Surely, they would require more than accompanying vocalists and instrumentalists in middle and high school, playing in the jazz band, and being the rehearsal pianist and a member of the pit band for the school musicals. Not even doing that for a summer stock production of *Godspell* and earning some money was likely to be enough. But playing in modern day's greatest Dixieland jazz band, hmmm...I'd like to say I had a chance.

Preservation Hall Jazz Band came to play in Chandler, Arizona in the late spring of my senior year in college. Anytime they were scheduled to play in our state, my family and I were there in the audience, tapping our feet to the contagious music. Seeing the band made the two and a half hour drive to the valley where my mother lived well worth it. This time around, my mother, my grandmother "Grammie", my stepfather Gavin, and I held the tickets to a blissful evening. It was likely to be our last outing together for some time since my graduation was looming, and I had vague plans to move back east, certainly not to stay in Arizona. I interviewed for practice when the big recruiters came to NAU, but had already decided that I did not want to work for a large company. In other words, I had very few restrictions on me; I was limited only by my imagination and determination, and I've always had plenty of both.

As we waited in the concert hall, we leafed through the playbills, reading about the musicians who were performing that night. Preservation Hall nearly always has a black musician or two who is in his 90's and has been playing forever. These men are so remarkable in terms of their talent and their history and the changes they've lived through. Now they're sought after and well paid performers, but there was a time they wouldn't have been permitted on the stage or in the audience. The younger musicians have had the privilege of growing up in musical families and having these old men as their mentors. I had the utmost respect for all of them, but there was one name on the playbill that elicited far stronger feelings, not just from me, but from my family as well.

Wendell Brunious. That was the villain's name, at least according to two characters in this story, but I knew differently. He was a Pied Piper with his Dixieland music, and, in my fantasy, I could have followed him anywhere. Life gets interesting when fantasies have the opportunity to become reality. A more alluring villain it is difficult to imagine, the confident, casual approach, the smart attire, the horn by his right leg, and that smooth voice, creamy as the inside of a Napoleon and just as tempting.

And, at age 40 give or take a few years, Wendell, our villain, was considered a young man. My mother and I have never shared the same taste in men, but Wendell was one we could agree on, despite the fact that he was considerably younger than she was, and he was considerably older than I. We both conceded he was an exception we were willing to make. My grandmother tutted and clucked over us, and Gavin made snide remarks about him, but they couldn't shake our admiration. As expected, the playbill listed Wendell as the trumpet player, primary vocalist and band leader. I do believe he was the best they ever had. He had a natural way with the audience, an intimate way of speaking to the listeners, as if he were winking at them all in confidence. He was a fine storyteller and did his duty of bringing Mardi Gras wherever they went. He carried his six foot frame with dignity but also just the perfect amount of slouching to give him an irresistible devil-may-care aura. His shirtsleeves were rolled up at the cuffs showing off well-toned forearms, and the fit of his chinos matched the relaxed way he wore life. His skin was the color of café au lait due to his Creole ancestry. He had a super slow smile and a sensual mouth, and, damn, he knew how to play that trumpet. He could make it swing, sing, moan, and produce the clearest tone. Leaning back and blowing on that horn skyward with his knees slightly bent and hips cocked forward, he cut quite a figure. Whether he was playing his horn or singing, his love of the music swept the room clear of everything but the notes, the rhythms and the lyrics.

We had good seats close to the stage, and during the concert, Wendell tossed bead necklaces into the audience in the Mardi Gras tradition. He looked at me and threw some directly to me. I claimed that he recognized me from my performance after a previous concert of theirs when I was about seventeen. My mother, I'm sure, claimed that they were meant for her, and my grandmother scoffed and told us, "Nonsense, he has a girl in every port." Gavin wisely stayed out of it. The concert concluded in the tradition of Preservation Hall Jazz Band and the imitation of a second line, whereby Wendell and some of the other jazz musicians who played easily portable instruments began marching through the aisles of the hall, winding their way throughout, joined by enthusiasts who danced along behind them. I was certainly not going to be held back by the less captivated in my party. I joined the merry group as they paraded past our row and followed along knowing our destination was the stage. I was a veteran. The merriness and dancing continued onstage until the last note sounded. Then everybody got a chance to interact with the band, shaking hands and telling them how much they enjoyed the performance. The band members signed autographs and chatted. I spoke to a young white man not much older than I named Ben Jaffe and the fairly young black drummer and asked how they got involved with the band. I was genuinely interested, but it also killed time while I waited to talk to Wendell.

Finally, he detangled himself from his other admirers and joined us. He said that he was glad I caught the beads because he'd thrown them for me. He remembered me from their last performance in Arizona because, after the show while I was on stage, I mentioned that I was a ragtime pianist and that I had seen Sweet Emma when I was 13 at Preservation Hall in N'awleans. He said, pulling out the piano bench for me, "Well, here, play me something, and I chose "Heliotrope Bouquet" by Scott Joplin and Louis Chauvin, one of my favorite rags. They were impressed and noted that it was in a difficult key. Then they suggested that I play the "Maple Leaf Rag," and they joined in. It was a neat experience. So, despite my grandmother's claim that there was a girl in every port, I knew there wasn't a girl like me. Ben, Joe the drummer, and I told Wendell that we had been talking about how one gets into playing with the band, and he invited me to walk backstage with him so we could continue talking about it. It was too great an opportunity to miss, so I didn't give a thought to my waiting family. They knew how musicians were after a show.

We walked back into the green room where he offered me a soda from a waiting iced tub of them, and then we proceeded to his dressing room, talking all the while. He apologized for rushing but said that they had their bus waiting outside to take them to the next gig in a neighboring state. I don't remember what I was wearing anymore, but my mother probably does, because according to her, she just caught a glimpse of it before the door to his dressing room slammed shut. She had come to see what was keeping me. She knocked loudly on the door and was admitted as he warmly greeted her and explained again about having to rush because the bus was waiting outside, and by this time, running. Of course, if we wanted to get on the bus with him, he said, we could keep on talking until the next show.

Right about then, Wendell responded to a sharp rap on the door of the dressing room which revealed Gavin on the other side, looking rather put out. Apparently, out in the concert hall, the sweepers had come out, and then they were beginning to turn off the lights while he sat there with my 86 year old grandmother, wondering what had become of us. My grandmother, thinking the same thoughts as my mother had been, said "We'd better go check up on her." She had trailed after Gavin who also claimed to have caught just a glimpse of my mother's outfit before the door to Wendell's dressing room slammed shut.

Since the concert hall was dark, we all followed along after Wendell out the side door towards the running bus.

The rest of my family started walking towards the parking lot and Gavin's car, but I stopped by the bus with Wendell. They started calling back to me, but I ignored them. This was not a time I wanted to rush. The bus and the lifestyle, not to mention Wendell, had this magnetic pull towards them, and I can imagine still with little effort how easy it would have been to climb on that bus and start my life as a Dixieland jazz band musician with the famous Preservation Hall. My family might have missed me, but they still could have seen me every time we came to play in the state.

Instead, Wendell and I hugged and kissed goodbye, and I turned my dancing feet towards the parking lot and my nervous family, clutching in my hand his personal card with his address and home phone number. I knew that whenever I did get to N'awleans again, I would have the best personal tour guide a girl could ask for, one who would know where to go for the best Dixieland jazz, and my "in" should I ever decide to become a Dixieland jazz band musician. After I reluctantly managed to climb into our car, and we headed back towards my grandmother's apartment, Gavin started griping about how late it was and how my mother and I had just left them sitting in the auditorium, until my mother and I demanded that he turn the car around and go back so we could get on the bus and be with some fun company. My mother claimed she needed to accompany me to make sure I didn't get into trouble. He was nearly ready to dispense with us, but unfortunately, we had my grandmother once again looking out for our best interests.

I have been reunited happily with Wendell at other concerts on the East Coast sans chaperones, and am still looking forward to my eventual trip to N'awleans. If indeed he does have a girl in every port, I am more than happy to be the one here.

The Summer of '55

Jackie Pruden was sure that the summer of 1955 promised to be the best one yet. As school was drawing to a close, he counted down the days until he was free from restriction; free to play baseball, free to run around outside until it got dark, free to stay up late, and free to hang out with his cousin Jimmie, who lived across the street and was two years older. Jackie filled those summer days with activities that would delight any ten and a half year old boy. In addition to Little League, he fished with his buddies in the Rockaway River, rode his bike to Lake Hiawatha and swam, played badminton with Jimmie, and there were always the old standbys of hide-and-seek and guns.

The nights were just as much fun as the days. The Good Humor truck (a Chevy pickup with an insulated square cooler in the back of it filled with dry ice, Dixie cups, and ice cream bars) jingled its way past the front doors as the dinner dishes were being cleared. Then, perhaps best of all, the pesticide trucks would drive through the neighborhood spraying the aromatic clouds of DDT for the pure enjoyment of little boys riding fast behind them on their bicycles. What better stuff could there be! It not only killed mosquitos but provided a perfumed challenge to try to keep up with the sprayers. Who could ride the fastest and the furthest, all the while breathing those thick bluish heavenly vapors?

After dark, Jackie's parents might watch TV with him, that is if the black and white picture ensconced in a heavy wood cabinet would come on after its two to three minute warm-up. They enjoyed the Perry Como Show, Jackie Gleason's Variety Show and the Honeymooners, Nat King Cole, Uncle Miltie and the Texaco Star Theatre, Abbott and Costello, and Jack Benny. Jack Pruden rooted for the New

York Giants and his son followed suit. They were not pleased that the Brooklyn Dodgers were playing such a great season. Jimmie rubbed it in after every winning game.

Weekends meant Jack had time off with his family, perhaps indulging his son and nephew with a game of Running Bases or taking his wife Helen, Jackie, and Robbie, Jackie's three year old baby brother, for a ride in the new car. The '55 green Chevy coupe with a white top was the first car the family had ever bought. Jack had always driven a company car, a respectable sedan, but the latest Kasco dog food truck with its bright yellow paint job and stripes radiating out from the center of its logo drove him to make the investment. Jackie also looked forward to the weekends because his grandparents came to visit from Bayonne and always brought gifts for the boys. Unfortunately, they spent every other weekend across the street at Jimmie's house, so on the weekends they were due at Jackie's, he was overcome with anticipation, asking what they'd brought him before he even uttered a greeting.

Yes, the summer of 1955 was looking very good indeed, but the best part of all was the vacation to the Jersey shore. Every year, Jackie's and Jimmie's families rented a house near the ocean for a week. But this year, the vacation was going to be better than ever! They were renting a house in Seaside Park for two whole weeks! The boys loved playing baseball, but they were ready for the Little League season to end so that they could leave for the real vacation. Everybody was going to be there: Jack and Helen, Jimmie's parents Frank and Doris, their grandparents from Bayonne, Jimmie's Uncle Carl, and, of course, little Robbie.

The boys were filled with anticipation as they arrived with their family at a two-story colonial cedar shake brown house built in the early 20th century. Its natural siding was weathered from the surrounding water—the ocean was a couple of blocks away, and it was even closer to the bay. It was a perfect location for Jackie and Jimmie! They went to the pier and the bay to fish and crabbed with cages. Sometimes the grown-ups rented a boat for the family for half a day. Their grandmother Agnes took the boys to see the King & I in the theater where James Dean was also playing in East of Eden. The streets were lively with the sounds of the newest hits: Bill Haley singing Rock Around the Clock, Little Richard with Tutti Frutti, Frank Sinatra crooning Love and Marriage, and Al Hibbler performing Unchained Melody. The boys were also on the lookout for the coolest cars of the summer, the Ford Fairlane, '55 Chevy Corvette, and '55 Chevy BelAir with a V-8 engine (brand new to Chevy that year.) It was a good summer indeed! When they weren't at the beach, the bay, or on the pier, the boys played whiffle ball in the street with a thin wooden bat which broke the balls all the time.

The summer nights at the shore were golden too. Two or three times a week, Jimmie and Jackie went to the boardwalk. To this day, there is no place anywhere that can rival the boardwalk at the Jersey shore! The boys were given $1.00 each which would buy 3 rides at 25¢ apiece and one slice of thin-crusted, gooey pizza, the best in the country. Their favorite rides were the whip and the bumper cars. Jimmie also liked the fun house with the laughing lady outside; she guffawed hysterically in this silky, loose-fitting dress, but Jackie thought she was rather creepy. He didn't want to be teased by Jimmie so he would find himself boarding the little car, trying to control his shivering, as they lurched through the doors into the dark of the fun house. He was relieved when they returned to the crowded boardwalk, the salty night air, the amusement park lights, and the scents of funnel cake and pretzels.

It was a fantastic vacation until the evening the grown-ups decided to have a night out on the town. They didn't often have a chance to go out all together. Carl, Uncle Frank's brother, lived in Ohio and made his living playing the trumpet in a big band. He was sociable and liked to make people laugh. The boys liked him because, although he teased them a bit, he was funny and always respectful of them too. However, on this night, they were feeling rather resentful—staying close to home was one thing, staying in to babysit three-year-old Robbie was quite another.

The evening was not going poorly—it was about 9 o'clock at night, and Robbie was upstairs sound asleep. But there was no TV in the rental house, the radio was not on, and Jackie and Jimmie had already played countless games of both regular and Chinese checkers. Jimmie picked up the funny pages to amuse himself, but Jackie hated reading. He scowled as he sat nearby, repeatedly thwacking a baseball in his left hand into his gloved right hand. Jimmie turned the page. Jackie glowered in his direction and thwacked louder.

Jimmie raised his gaze just enough to see Jackie's face over the top of the newspaper and asked, "Geez, man, what gives? You're being a pest."

Jackie exploded, "I'm so bored, I can't stand it!"

"We've got to do something," he whined. They sat for a moment.

"What if we play a prank?" Jimmie said.

Jackie smiled, "Okay, but on who? It can't be my dad. I don't want to get in trouble."

Jimmie smiled back, "How about on Robbie? Nobody will even know but us."

"What if he tells, he always tells," said Jackie.

"We'll just say he dreamed it," Jimmie grinned.

"Should we stick his hand in a bowl of warm water so he'll wet the bed?" Jackie suggested. "Or how about we hide in the closet and make scary noises?"

Jimmie said, "I think I've got a better idea. Come with me."

The door to Carl's bedroom squeaked on its hinges when Jimmie turned the knob. He clicked the switch on the lamp, glanced around and said, "Bingo, we're in business."

Jackie followed his gaze where it had come to rest on an alligator leather case, all black except for the brass clasps. Jimmie flicked them open and lifted Carl's trumpet out of its protective hollow. He took the mouthpiece out next and screwed it in.

"What are you doing with that?" Jackie asked as he trailed Jimmie back into the living room.

"This is it," Jimmie said. "We're going to shock the hell out of him by blowing this right into his ear. He'll probably wake up screaming, but, by the time he looks around, he won't see anybody or anything there."

"That's cool." Jackie replied. "You'll have to be the one who blows, though. I don't know how to play the trumpet."

"Look, I'll show you."

Jimmie first demonstrated how to hold the trumpet. "You don't even have to press down any buttons," he explained. "You just have to purse your lips in the mouthpiece, keep them that way and blow as hard as you can. Pretend you're an elephant—there's a reason they say elephants trumpet. That's it, just make like an elephant. Here, you can try it with just the mouthpiece, but I don't think we should go for the full effect until you're up there. We don't want to wake him up before the grand finale."

"But aren't you going to do it?" Jackie asked.

"No, I think it should be you. If we both go up there, he might hear us coming. He's more used to you since you share a room at home. Go on, I dare you."

Jimmie remained downstairs while Jackie tiptoed upstairs to the landing, trying not to giggle. He slowly eased through the doorway to Robbie's bedroom until he was standing next to his sleeping brother. The splash of light from the hallway revealed the easy rise and fall of Robbie's belly in contrast to Jackie's quickened breathing. Jackie could smell the hot, slightly musty old house smells as he gathered his breath into his chest. He brought the mouthpiece to his lips as he bent over and positioned the bell beside Robbie's ear. His slick fingers curled around the gleaming brass instrument. He drew in one final gulp of air until he could feel it reach all the way into his ears and up to the top of his head. Holding that immense breath, he pursed his lips inside the mouthpiece and thought, "Just make like an elephant."

Then he let loose on that horn! A brief burst of sound shattered the silence as Jackie tried to win the battle of blowing over laughing. He could hear Jimmie whooping it up down below as he dropped down out of sight beside the bed, not wanting to be the first thing Robbie saw when he started shrieking. But all was silent, even downstairs. Jackie decided to have another go at it; surely two times would do the trick. He took another huge breath, clamped his moist hands back over the trumpet, puckered his lips, inserted them into the mouthpiece again, and encircled Robbie's ear with the bell. Once more he blew as hard as he could, and then hit the floor trying not to laugh. His anticipation was short-lived, though. Jackie peered over the edge of the mattress at Robbie who only stirred a little bit, turned over, and went back to sleep. Giggling anyway, Jackie started back out of the bedroom. He and Jimmie would just have to find something else to occupy themselves.

Jackie couldn't believe his brother didn't wake up. What a sound sleeper! He reached the top of the stairs, still giggling a little, holding the trumpet by the mouthpiece he had just wailed into. Whether it was from the impact as Jackie stepped down one, then two stairs, or perhaps from the lubrication of his spit, the trumpet detached itself from the mouthpiece. Jackie couldn't do anything but stand frozen on the third step down, watching Carl's trumpet do its slow motion descent down the wooden stairs. The only sound that emanated from his mouth was a sharp indrawn breath, "Huuunh!"

In contrast, the trumpet hit all kinds of non-musical notes. Clang went the bell which hit the steps first. Clink went the valves on the edge of a riser. Clank was the place where the mouthpiece used to be. Clang, clink, clank once more, and a final clunk as the trumpet bounced off the wall at the foot of the stairs, finally coming to rest. Jimmie couldn't see it from his seat on the couch, but he could hear the unmistakable strikes of metal against wood. Reluctantly, he came to stand in the hallway as Jackie's paralysis lost its hold.

"What the hell happened?" Jimmie demanded.

"I didn't mean it. It just slipped off. I couldn't stop it. I'm sorry, I didn't mean it," Jackie moaned. "One minute everything was fine, and the next..." He didn't need to finish the thought.

The boys gingerly picked up Carl's trumpet to inspect the damage, the mouthpiece still dangling from Jackie's left hand. The curved part of the trumpet near where the mouthpiece belonged sported a new and very noticeable dent. There was no way they could fix the damage and no way they could hide it. Slowly they trudged into the kitchen to assess their options.

Jimmie and Jackie sank into the kitchen chairs and brainstormed ways out of their situation. Maybe they could run away. Maybe they could hide the trumpet. Maybe they could pretend it was stolen. Blaming it on Robbie did not seem like a likely story, either. In the end, they decided their best option was to write a letter of apology and be in bed asleep before the grown-ups came home. Jimmie wrote the letter, sharing the responsibility as the oldest (and as their parents probably intuited, the instigator), and they placed it on the kitchen table in a prominent position.

"What do you think is going to happen to us?" asked Jackie. "I really don't like getting spanked."

"We'll probably get grounded, you know they won't let us go do things, or we'll have to go to bed early. Something like that," Jimmie replied.

"What if they won't let us out of our rooms for the rest of vacation?" Jackie said.

"Oh, I don't think it will be that bad. I'm not looking forward to facing Uncle Carl though. I know how much he loves that trumpet. He's had it a long time. He told me he doesn't want a new one because they've been through a lot together," said Jimmie.

"Do you think it can be fixed? Do you think we're going to have to work to pay for it to be fixed? I don't get much allowance," Jackie groaned.

"We'll have to wait and see. I'm sure they'll be plenty mad. Let's get to sleep before they get here," urged Jimmie.

Feeling sick at heart, the boys headed up to bed, dreading what the morning would bring. {Interestingly, neither boy remembers major repercussions, and oddly, neither boy remembers any details about the aftermath. Nobody knows what became of that letter either.}

The summer of 1955 approached its end, and if two boys returned to Parsippany from the Jersey shore a little older, a little wiser, and a little more respectful of other people's belongings, it has sadly gone unmentioned until now. Let's just hope as they become parents and then grandparents, that they remember the power of temptation and mischief, the magic of summer vacations, and the unparalleled times spent at the Jersey shore and go a little easy on the punishments too!

R. C. S.

On Nature

What is natural in this
mixed up world of ours?
Killing each other
because we do not share
the same fantasy religion
cannot be the whole answer.
All religions are false,
deep in everyone's heart
is that knowledge,
only we cling to them
because we are too weak
to face reality.
Infidel! Heretic!
Heathen! Atheist!
All fanatics yell the same
nonsense.
All fanatics
be they
Muslim, Catholic or Protestant
Buddhist or Hindu
are wrong,
all are unnatural.

Too Simple to be Believed

The world has been here
forever,
and it will be here
forever more.
Beginningless and endless.

Yet some need to
believe in a beginning
and some,
a god to begin it,
to believe in the supernatural
for which there is no evidence.

Rather than believe in the real world,
that is,
they need to believe in a god
that cannot be.

Cogito ergo Sum

Cold hard reality is a myth.
Reality is hot, squishy and
never ending.
Not for the timid.
And hence religions and other
empty diversions are created
for those who can't take Reality
straight, and hot
and who can't face themselves
or the world.
How sad.
Some of us enjoy Reality
and the myriad and
limitless possibilities
only IT can provide.
Rejoice in the real world.

Sarah

Age 15

My Marching Heart

Do you hear it?
The sound of my beating heart?
A simple thump, thump, lulling me to sleep
my only comfort, my only lullaby
Hold me close so that you may hear
my lullaby and that I may hear yours
A constant drum beat played by a tireless
Drummer that can never sleep
for if he does, I will fall asleep with him
and he will never wake up to play the rhythm again
so lend me your ear, so that you may hear
the beating of my heart, a simple thump, thump

W

To My Granddaughter

I gave you a kiss today.
I didn't send it - I put it away.
 In a small, tin box
 Wrapped warm with a hug
 Which will keep it snug, like
A bug in a rug.
1 am taking it with me
On my walk in the park
To hide it, you see
Just for a lark
In a place where children play
 It will lie in rest
   Until ¬–
      Until, the day that you find it!
We'll go for a walk
   And take the dog
Past the old white birch and the hollow log
   And I'll give you a hint where the box might be
You'll find it I know ¬
   And look inside - to find
      The kiss ¬-
         And ¬
            And - a little surprise!

Vagrant Thoughts

Like tumbleweeds,
Blown by the wind
Across the vacant landscape of the mind.
They come,
From whence, unknown, to whither, soon blown.

Max

He lets me sleep, napping beside me.
Awake at last -but
Not a day for man or beast!
Wind chill to 20 degree and colder!
Duty calls -a walk? A walk!
Into the truck with a bound...
An eager whine, almost a whinneyl
Stay boy –stay boy – OK go.
What a gift he gives me!
This day... Alive!

Epitaph for Spring

The wind whispers to me a silent song,
The days now short, will soon be long.
But short or long, it is fast they fly
So use them well -for we all must die
And the days that are short,
And the days that are long,
All of them will then be gone.

In Sickness and In Health

I am scared to death in my very soul
what will happen to my love and me?
All these years, side by side
what will happen to my love and me?
Family and friends are loyal and kind
but what will happen to my love and me?
I pray to God to see us through
what will happen to my love and me?

Dian West

Time Lapse

Traveling South
in early May
like time-lapse photography
the trees
leaf out
colors changing
from gray and rust
to bright green and rosy red
with touches of white
showing the promise
of rebirth
for Northern New England.

Purple Shirts

the morning mist is
filled with purple balloons
over the heads of
purple-shirted people with
different stories
different memories
different cultures
but all sharing the
same pain
same heartbreak
same hope
that no one else
will be a
purple-shirted person
touched by the
horror of
Pancreatic Cancer

Go Train Go

Curly headed
Thunder Foot
runs
to the bookshelf
brings back
Go Train Go
Thomas saves the day
faster than fast
Thunder Foot
runs
brings back
Go Train Go
Thomas saves the day
faster than fast
Curly headed
Thunder Foot
brings back
Go Train Go
faster than fast
Thomas once again
saves the day
and Thunder Foot's
Grandma
smiles as she reads

A Faraway Place

Memories line the wall
of friends
lost and held dear from
wounds
received in the jungle
of a faraway place

Scars mar the smooth skin
of his back
reminders of long ago
wounds
received in the jungle
of a faraway place

Nightmares mar the peace
of sleep
keeping alive the
wounds
received in the jungle
of a faraway place

Perrin

A small boy fills my heart
He smiles and I beam back
His laughter is
the most beautiful music
I have ever heard

New

I bought a new dress today
I have a wonderful dress
That I love
But
I bought a new dress
That isn't in a picture
With my first love
A dress that will be
For the here and now
Offering hope for the future

New Beginning

a first date
a glass of wine
a chat
a bowl of soup
a kiss blown in a parking lot
a promise of another date
a smile on my face

Spring Tease

Spring teases.
Whispering warmly
she lifts her snowy skirts
revealing seductive green patches
and garden edges aching to be tilled.
Then she blows cold
covering up in a cloak of new snow.

Carol White

Midsummer Night's Dreaming

I love summer. I live for it. For about 30 years or so I have spent the summer solstice in my garden, usually with friends, watching the sun set, the fireflies flit forth, and the pale moon come glimmering in the sky.

Sometimes we were a wild bunch. Oh yes, with cookies, lemonade and iced tea. In the years when I had hundreds of rosebushes we would walk barefoot on rose petals and have masses of roses in vases, buckets, and once or twice, we stuffed pillows with rose petals and slept on them that night. Cleopatra, eat your heart out!

At midsummer I feel sorry for people in more southern areas where night falls like a window shade. Bang-daylight's gone. In the days of the rose garden I kept thinking that it might, just might, be possible for a unicorn to appear out of the cool, blue, firefly-lit twilight. None ever did, but now I think they may prefer to make a more striking entrance from the hemlock-scented darkness of the northern forest surrounding my rather small clearing. They'd certainly be welcome.

I think anyone living at this latitude feels the same way about summer: make the most of it. When I visited cousins in Husqvarna, Sweden in midsummer (the only possible time to spend time there according to my aunt), the light lingered on until after 11:00 p.m., as families all over Sweden celebrated summer with huge meals of crayfish and boiled potatoes, eaten picnic style in yards or parks with paper lanterns shaped like suns and moons dancing overhead. (And akvavit, let's not forget the akvavit, true Scandinavian firewater.)

Oddly enough, the crayfish reminded me of home. The native Swedish crayfish all succumbed to some dread disease many years ago and were replaced by stocks from the U.S. and, of all places, Turkey. But guess where the best and strongest crayfish came from? Yep, right here in New Hampshire. I travelled how many hundreds of miles to eat New Hampshire crayfish boiled with dill?

I haven't had it since. Perhaps if a bottle of akvavit turned up?

Like many New Hampshire folks, the Swedes are mad gardeners. I know the English have the reputation as a nation of gardeners, but even in Sweden's capital city the most modern, black glass pyramid of an apartment building had pots and pots of veggies and flowers burgeoning on ultra-modern balconies.

Little red garden houses in the middle of a garden plot are ubiquitous on the outskirts of the cities. Those who can have slightly larger red houses in the countryside or on the scattered islands of the tideless Baltic. No one stays inside on a summer evening.

Just like home. On the solstice evening this year I grilled my dinner on the deck, drank something fizzy, and sat watching the light slowly fade. Here in the Lakes area I can always count on volleys of fireworks as darkness finally falls. The fishermen who stay out on the lake, where it is light long after darkness falls under the trees, call to their friends on the shore, homing in on their docks and moorings.

As the dark deepens, stillness comes. If I sit quietly enough, long enough, I often think I just might see, well, probably not a unicorn, but the bears enjoying these long summer twilights, too.

Fall Planting, Winter Dreaming

Some of my best ideas have come to me as I relax in my hammock, recovering from prying up rocks, digging holes and spreading heavy mulch. This particular brainstorm came as I contemplated an enormous apple tree under full sail of pink and white blossoms.

Underneath the tree, hellebores prospered near the trunk, and the drip line was hemmed with lamium. Very nice. But it lacked something. It lacked strength. It lacked purple, that's what it lacked. Very good. Problem identified, now a solution. What would fill the intermediate space, provide the color, and be low maintenance. "Yes, please, low maintenance."

Well, crocuses, of course.

Like most really good ideas, fulfillment came at a cost. I diligently saved my pennies, trimmed here and there, and by the end of July placed my order for 1000 purple and purple-and-white-striped crocus. Every time I looked at that apple tree I had to smile. It was going to be great.

I waited, waited, and waited some more. My corms were due the second week of September. I gave them an extra two weeks, then called the vendor.

The bulbs had been sent on schedule. Was I sure I hadn't received them? Okay, I'll never win prizes for my powers of observation, but I'm pretty sure I'd have noticed a thousand crocus bulbs on my front steps.

Another week later the package was located in upper New York state. I received constant notification of its inchwormlike progress from New York to Michigan. (Michigan?) From there to Connecticut and thence to Massachusetts.

Good grief! When the poor cardboard carton arrived another five days later, it looked as if it had been the focal point of a buffalo stampede. Somehow the corms hadn't been smashed, and there were still exactly 1000 of them.

I placed them, one by one, in the soft, prepared earth, viewed the arrangement from all sides, did some rearranging, and began to plant. The sun set and still I planted. My back protested vigorously. My knees sang counterpoint. Still I planted.

The more frost-proof mosquitoes sang in my ears. I really thought about quitting, but I just couldn't leave my carefully arranged crocus. I planted until every last corm had been lovingly tucked into its appointed spot.

Then I discovered that I really, truly, couldn't get up. Nothing was working. Communicating, yes. Loudly. But I couldn't force my back and knees to get me off the ground. What to do?

Yelling for help was out. I'd collect frost first. I rolled and crawled to the spading fork and used it to lever myself up. I then lurched the interminable distance between my garden and the house a superlative imitation of Quasimodo, if I do say so myself. The next morning, I was unable to get out of bed.

The reminder of that evening in the garden stayed with me through the winter. Ah, but so did my mental images of the apple tree billowing over its carpet of purple crocus and hellebores. Ibuprofen and my imagination were my soul's support throughout that long and snowy winter. I imagined my crocus, safe under the snow, putting out roots. Then as the snow melted and the soil warmed I made a dozen trips a day looking for new shoots.

The apple buds swelled. The hellebores bloomed. The only activity where the crocus had been planted was the appearance of dozens of dark, round, little holes. Holes where vole families, vole clans and entire tribes had wintered on my crocus.

My friend in the Air National Guard thought I was perhaps overreacting when I asked if he could arrange a practice air strike on my apple tree. Hah! Norse mythology had a serpent gnawing at the root of the tree that supported the world. I have news. The mythologists had it wrong. It was a vole.

I tried everything. Voles blew bubbles with gum dropped into their holes and made nests of human hair gleaned from the hairdresser's floor. Rototilling merely meant redecorating to the voles.

"Nice place you've got here."
"Yes, the landlady just rearranged the roof and walls."

I also rearranged things. I moved. I have never planted another crocus, I have no apple tree. I encourage the feared fisher cats to come and prowl my flower beds. My only tangible memory of that hammock-induced vision is the twinge I get in my back any time I pick up a shovel.

Drawing by Pamela Doherty

Hum along with me

While I can't say that I have a favorite bird, hummingbirds are certainly one of my favorites: colorful, fearless, and busy. I hear their twittering constantly as I work in the garden. I've watched adults court and females raise the newly fledged babies.

A year ago we had a female with two little ones flying from basket to basket of colorful flowers on my porch. Mom would twitter at the little ones, then fly off to another kind of flower and they'd fly after her. After a few days the youngsters wouldn't respond so quickly to her, staying with their chosen blossoms while Mom zipped away.

Mom was unusual in that she seemed curious about us, the human residents. When we sat on the deck for lunch she would come and circle under the umbrella, watching us as she twirled. It made me positively dizzy. If I worked in the yard, she was always there. When I worked among the phlox she would come close and squeak at me, probably protecting her favorite food. I decided it was just as well that I didn't understand Hummingbird.

In late August I started having my morning tea in the garden, wedging myself in among the zinnias small pink ones, as closely as I could. One morning as I sipped, I heard the familiar twittering and the "whum" of hummingbird wings close to my ear. I didn't move, but felt the swirl of air by my face and the incredible lightness of a hummingbird as she perched on my forearm and peered at me with her shiny black eyes.

She knew perfectly well I wasn't a plant, but chose to land there. Although she rested on my arm for only a moment, she then stayed inches from me, testing each of the pink zinnias before she flew off. This wasn't the first time I'd had a wild bird perch on me, but a hummingbird! I was thrilled.

For a few weeks each time I sat in the garden she would come, stay close while we observed each other, then zip off. When the hummingbirds disappeared to go south, I wished her well. Sadly, none of the females this year seem interested. I fear she has not returned.

However, a male hummingbird, a ruby-jeweled beauty, has taught me that I have underestimated his species. As a giant I assumed that such little creatures were probably not terribly bright, but this gentleman looks in my windows and recognizes the hummingbird feeder.

He started by greeting me when I hung the feeder out in the morning. Then he started displaying, hovering in front of the slider, as I walked toward it carrying the feeder. Now he twits and squeaks outside my kitchen window as I fill the feeder bottle. When I move away from the sink he zips around the corner of the house to the deck, hovering by the slider until I open the door and come out. He precedes me to the hanger for the feeder, and then flies off, not stopping to feed. Usually a female comes as soon as I step away. Then he zooms down from his perch in the nearby hemlock.

Is he waiting for me to bring out the "babe magnet?" Could this be one of the hatchlings I watched being trained last summer? A bird accustomed to the proximity of humans?

I'll never know, but I salute hummingbirds everywhere: birds as bright as their feathers.

Turning and Falling

Here we are again at the turn of another season. For me this a major point of the year; the harvests are in and the corn fields are stubble, haunted by mice and their kin.

Now I prize the rare days of October's bright blue weather, a gift worth sapphires. More accurately, they are days of rubies and topaz, citrines and garnets strewn across the hills. I revel in the days of golden sun and towering white clouds soaring over New Hampshire's mountains. These are the days brimming with life, and their brevity is a reminder to enjoy it while we can. Wring out the gusto!

It's true that every lake and pond has a frame of reds, oranges and gold to bronze. Quiet summer days are gone. Blustery days bring whitecaps riding on the larger lakes, but there are those few still mornings when the colors are doubled at the water's edge. Paddling quietly, moving on the water's surface, I can cross reflections that disappear as I come to them, beckoning me on like a mirage in the desert.

But the mountains are where autumn's treasure is on full display. Miles of roads and trails wind through our White Mountains to give unparalleled views over thousands of acres of color and an incredible variety of textures and topographies. I love to move through the deciduous forests from the bright softness of comparatively lush growth to the more austere, rocky slopes.

In these mountains every trail is cut by streams, clear water running from the rocks, seeping or leaping as it obeys gravity and finds its way down the slopes. The sounds of water offer a counterpoint to the rustle of leaves.

As I gain height the evergreens become more prevalent. The breeze has a more whispered voice. Shade holds a chill, but in the sunshine warmth melts through my jacket, sinking into my body. On such a sunny, slightly damp day, I climb higher still, where the balsams fur the rocky slopes, to enjoy the incomparable scent of balsam riding on the cool breeze.

I turn and look out to the northwest to the huge U-shaped valleys where once glaciers hung above like solid clouds and rivers of glacial silt scoured the land. I try to imagine it. I close my eyes and feel the cold wind, chill from the mile-high ice, blowing past me. I open them again and it is our own bright and bold October in the mountains.

The views out over some of the glacier-carved valleys give a tempting idea of what the hawks and eagles see as they ride the thermals up the mountainsides. A huge bowl of brilliance, hemmed in by the old worn mountains of New Hampshire's ranges.

I see how the colors follow ridges and valleys and notice the flaring scarlet of the swamp maples clustering where their roots trail into the dampest soils. Following the jewel-box of deciduous colors trailing up into the dark, spiky evergreens, I see how the evergreens infiltrate the gray of bedrock and talus slopes. I long for wings.

Previews of November's bleak days come at the very tops of windward slopes where October's gales have already scoured away the leaves on the few dwarfed hardwoods. Even the hardy evergreens are bent and stunted, edging rock outcrops worn as smooth as pavement.

Still, even in the grey of old rock, I sometimes find an echo of autumn's colors, a hint of deep red, where actual garnets lie in the stone. I retreat quickly back to the next lower level patting the balsam needles as I pass, hoping to keep their fragrance lingering with me at least until I get home.

These October days of gold and garnet will be my treasure box in winter; one that I will open when the grey and cold gets oppressive. They will see me through until the next turning of the year.

Made in the USA
Charleston, SC
09 March 2012